Virtue Seeds

ACTIVITIES TO EXPLORE VIRTUES

By Elaheh Bos

www.plantlovegrow.com
©Plantlovegrow 2016
©Elaheh Bos 2016

ISBN: 978-0-9810556-2-6

Legal Deposit, Library and Archives
Canada, 2016

MW01130019

Table of Contents

1. Cooperation	1
2. Compassion	3
3. Courage	5
4. Creativity	7
5. Determination	9
6. Forgiveness	11
7. Generosity	13
8. Gentleness	15
9. Helpfulness	17
10. Honesty	19
11. Joyfulness	21
12. Kindness	23
13. Moderation	25
14. Modesty	27
15. Patience	29
16. Respect	31
17. Responsibility	33
18. Service	35
19. Trust	37
20. Unity	39
Activity pages	41

plant
love
grow

How to use the Virtue Activity Guide

This guide was created as a tool to help teach virtues through group activities, discussions and games. These activities provide learning and discussion opportunities between parents, children, and educators.

Quotes:

Special space has been provided for inspirational quotes. These can be religious, spiritual, scientific, or beautiful sayings that you create to focus your energy on the virtue you are exploring. These quotes can be memorized and are there to provide inspiration.

What you need in your tool box:

- Paper towels.
- Glue (appropriate to age, glue stick is often the easiest).
- Craft paper, magazines, recycled paper, white papers for drawing.
- Scissors (age appropriate).
- Pencil, crayons or markers (what I call colouring or drawing tools).
- Paint and paintbrushes.
- A box full of things you would normally recycle.
- Copies of the activity and colouring pages (enough for everyone).

We suggest giving each child a binder for them to keep their finished projects or to write about the activities. Ask them to personalize their binders.

Before starting any activity:

1. Discuss together three to five simple guidelines for the group to follow during the activities. These guidelines should be inspired by virtues and should focus on the desired behaviour.

2. Preparation is key. Choose the activity ahead of time and prepare your materials. Prepare your space. If you plan on using the virtue guide as part of a scheduled class, read all the activities ahead and add them to your calendar. Always make extra copies of the material you plan to use.

3. Create a routine around the activities. If you do them on a daily basis, arrange a specific time each day. If you do them on a weekly basis, do them on the same day if possible. Everyone will begin to anticipate the next activity with excitement.

4. Create roles and responsibilities to match the age of the children. This will be a great opportunity for them to learn responsibility, and will allow everyone to be involved and feel responsible for the success of the activity.

5. Focus on the process, not the outcome. Learning, spending time together, discussing what a virtue means to us, sharing our own stories and trying something new is more important than the results of an activity. Enjoy the process and discussions.

1. Cooperation

True or False - Discuss your choices:

Cooperation means getting other people to do your work for you.
True [ ] False [ ]

Cooperation means working together with other people.
True [ ] False [ ]

Good cooperation takes place when everyone feels happy about their contribution
and when everyone has made an effort to work together with others.
True [ ] False [ ]

When cooperating with others it is important to be bossy and tell others what to do.
True [ ] False [ ]

A beautiful quote about Cooperation: Write down a quote that you wish to memorize or remember.
If you cannot find a quote to inspire you, try coming up with your own.

Word Game:
Colour the words that show examples of Cooperation and discuss your choices.
Create sentences that show Cooperation using some of these words or combinations.

WORK TOGETHER	RUN	TRUST
BAKE ALONE	HAVE LUNCH	UNITE
TEAM UP	THINK ALOUD	TAKE A BATH

Come up with an example of someone practicing Cooperation.

Activity 1: Body in progress

NEED:

Large papers []
Drawing and
colouring tools   []

Take a long piece of paper and fold it into several sections so that each section folds into the next (like an accordion). Share how the goal of this activity is to draw a whole body (head, neck, shoulders and so on...). Each person can only draw one section of the body. There should be no talking or advice given while each person draws their part. Have the first person draw the head and then fold the paper to hide that part. Continue until the body is complete. If working with fewer people, take turns doing different parts. When the drawing is complete, open and admire. Talk about the experience. Would it have been easier if you could see what the others were drawing?

Activity 2: Animal matching

NEED:

Drawing and
colouring tools []
Large papers []
Scissors []

Cut a large piece of paper into smaller pieces. Everyone should have two small pieces of paper. Have everyone think of an animal, and without talking or sharing which animal was chosen, draw a part of that animal on one sheet of paper. Match all the pieces together and look at the new animal you have all created. How does the picture look? Now take your second piece of paper and this time pick an animal together and decide who is going to be responsible for drawing each part of the animal. Match all the pieces and share the results together. How does the picture look this time?

Discuss whether it was easier or harder to cooperate with others and what the benefits of cooperating were.

Ways to practice Cooperation:

❤ Do activities with friends and family.

❤ Share special projects with other people and make sure everyone has fun in the process.

❤ Play games where you have to cooperate with others.

2. Compassion

True or False - Discuss your choices:

Compassion means trying to understand what others may be going through.
True [ ] False [ ]

Having compassion means not letting other people get mad or feel hurt.
True [ ] False [ ]

Compassionate people always wear clothes with lots of pockets.
True [ ] False [ ]

We can show compassion by forgiving others for making mistakes and by being kind when others feel hurt or sad.
True [ ] False [ ]

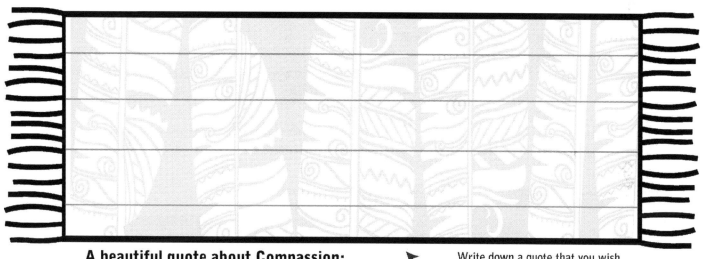

A beautiful quote about Compassion:

 Write down a quote that you wish to memorize or remember.
If you cannot find a quote to inspire you, try coming up with your own.

Word Game:

Colour the words that show examples of Compassion and discuss your choices.
Create sentences that show Compassion using some of these words or combinations.

SNEEZE	WEAR A HAT	SHOW EMPATHY
UNDERSTAND	SHOW CONCERN	LAUGH
EAT FOOD	ORDER A PIZZA	CARE FOR OTHERS

Come up with an example of someone practicing Compassion.

Activity 1: Walking in someone else's shoes

Read the following scenario together:
It is Monday morning and everyone is running late around
the house. A mother is trying to feed the baby and make sure
the 2 kids have their lunches. A father cannot find his important
paper. A baby is crying. One child has not finished his/her homework
and the other child is afraid of being teased at school.

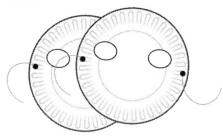

NEED:
Many different pairs of shoes
(different sizes if possible) []

Place the shoes around the room so that each person in the scenario
is represented by a pair of shoes. Go from one pair of shoes to the next and guess what that
person may be thinking, feeling or saying. Take turns putting on the different pairs of shoes.
Share your thoughts on the activity. How did it feel to be in someone else's shoes?
How can you show compassion for the different people in the scenario?

Activity 2: Mask of Compassion

NEED:
Paper plates
(2/participant) []
Paint and brushes []
Colouring tools []
Scissors []
String []
Tape []

Discuss what compassion is and how each one of us can have compassion
for others. Talk about other qualities or virtues that you need to have in
order to have compassion. Talk about what the opposite of compassion
might be. Draw two faces on your plates. On one plate draw a face showing
love and compassion and on the other draw a face showing anger or
frustration. Draw or paint the faces, cut out holes for the eyes and tape
some string on the sides to turn them into masks.

Create a short play about Compassion
using your masks.

Ways to practice Compassion:

♥ When you see other people in public looking sad or acting in certain ways, discuss
what could possibly be happening in their lives and how we can show compassion.

♥ Offer encouragement to any deeds of kindness and compassion shown, especially towards
friends, other siblings or family members.

♥ Make cards or bake cookies for someone who is sick or not feeling well. Have everyone
participate in the activity.

3. Courage

True or False - Discuss your choices:

We show courage when we do dangerous things that we are not allowed to do.
True [ ] False [ ]

We show courage when we do something that is very hard for us to do.
True [ ] False [ ]

We show courage when we do something even though we may be afraid to do it or think that we are not capable.
True [ ] False [ ]

We can show courage by bragging to others that we are not afraid of the dark.
True [ ] False [ ]

I am totally NOT afraid of vacuum cleaners...

A beautiful quote about Courage:
Write down a quote that you wish to memorize or remember. If you cannot find a quote to inspire you, try coming up with your own.

Word Game:
Colour the words that show examples of Courage and discuss your choices.
Create sentences that show Courage using some of these words or combinations.

BE DARING	MAKE ORIGAMI	CREATE A POEM
LEARN	BE BRAVE	WALK BAREFOOT
PICK FLOWERS	COOK	SING A SONG

Come up with an example of someone practicing Courage.

Activity 1: Courage Spiral
Have copies of page 41 made on card stock or thicker paper.

Discuss what courage means to you. Share how the spiral
on page 41 represents our journey of courage.
Before cutting the spiral write something that may help you get from FEAR
all the way to COURAGE. It could be a sentence, a series of steps or even
a poem. Write, decorate, and cut the spiral. Make a little hole and pass the
string through to hang it. Share your spiral with others.

Activity 2: Courage badge
Have copies of page 43 made on card stock or thicker paper.

Discuss what courage means to you and come up with your own
definition. Discuss how even the smallest acts can sometimes show
great courage. Make yourself different courage badges using the
models on page 43. Colour them, write different things on them
and use them as models to make as many as you want.

Using the glue gun or tape, carefully attach the badges to the clothing pin.
Create a ceremony in which everyone is awarded a badge of courage.
At this ceremony, share a personal story of courage and receive your courage badge.
Keep it somewhere safe as a reminder of the wonderful quality you have inside of you.

Ways to practice Courage:

💜 Make an effort to finish things that are hard for you.

💜 Make an effort to overcome fear or personal challenges.

💜 Read stories of courageous people.

💜 Assist someone else to be courageous by helping them finish a hard project.

4. Creativity

True or False - Discuss your choices:

Creativity is a way of doing things using our imagination. Sometimes it means looking at things in a different way or finding unusual ways of solving problems.
True [ ] False [ ]

We show that we are creative when we do silly things.
True [ ] False [ ]

Being creative means using your hands and your imagination to create things that are different and unique.
True [ ] False [ ]

You should always try your best to do everything like everyone else.
True [ ] False [ ]

A beautiful quote about Creativity:

Write down a quote that you wish to memorize or remember.
If you cannot find a quote to inspire you, try coming up with your own.

Word Game:

Colour the words that show examples of Creativity and discuss your choices.
Create sentences that show Creativity using some of these words or combinations.

BE ORIGINAL	PICK FLOWERS	WRITE A SONG
LEND A BOOK	BE RESOURCEFUL	TALK
IMAGINE	MAKE COOKIES	CREATE SOMETHING

Come up with an example of someone practicing Creativity.

Activity 1: Hidden colours

Long drying time – Prepare in advance.

Colour the entire paper with lots of different colours using the crayons. It is not necessary to create an image.
Rub the soap (do not wet the soap) over the entire paper. Paint the entire paper with black paint (use as little water as possible) and let dry. You can use a hair dryer to help speed up the drying time. With a toothpick or any other object, scratch a design through the black layer so the colourful colours underneath can be seen.

Share your creative artwork with others.

NEED:
Large papers []
Crayons [] MUST be wax crayons
Black paint []
Soap (bar not liquid) []
Toothpick or object to scratch []
Hair dryer
(can help speed up drying) []

Activity 2: Create your own product

NEED:

Page 45 []
Things from the recycling box
(mostly cans, boxes...) []
Any materials from around
the house []
(buttons, yarn, shells etc.)
Scissors []
Tape or glue []
Colouring tools []
Writing tools []
Other decorative items []

Use your imagination and what you have around to create a product based on yourself, your character, passions and virtues. For example, take an old tomato can and transform it into a can of kindness soup with unique ingredients.

Draw new packaging and create a new label for your product. Look at page 45 to inspire yourself from this product label or to create your own.

Nutritional Facts	
per 175 g	
Loyalty	5%
Courage	3%
Determination	4%
Sugar	7%
Responsibility	3%
Vitamine A	6%
Vitamine C	4%
Patience	8%
Kindness	4%
Compassion	3%
Proteins	1%
Love	6%
Self-discipline	13%
Respect	4%
Sucres	7%
Carbohydrates	0%
Vitamine D	6%
Vitamine E	4%
Trust	3%
Calcium	9%

Ways to practice Creativity:

♥ Look at things in different ways.

♥ Make your own toys and create your own games using what is around.

♥ Try to solve problems by looking at them from different angles.

♥ Have fun outside.

♥ Invent a new recipe.

5. Determination

True or False - Discuss your choices:

Determination is when we make an effort to finish something that is hard for us.
True [ ] False [ ]

We show determination when we stay upset for a very long time.
True [ ] False [ ]

When something takes a very long time to learn, or when we need a lot of courage and persistence to finish something hard and yet we still manage to complete it, then we show determination.
True [ ] False [ ]

We show determination when we eat a lot of food even if we are not hungry.
True [ ] False [ ]

A beautiful quote about Determination: Write down a quote that you wish to memorize or remember. If you cannot find a quote to inspire you, try coming up with your own.

Word Game:
Colour the words that show examples of Determination and discuss your choices.
Create sentences that show Determination using some of these words or combinations.

SHOW STRENGTH	PERSEVERE	BAKE
WILLPOWER	SMILE	START A FIGHT
PICK FLOWERS	UNDERSTAND	LEARN

Come up with an example of someone practicing Determination.

Activity 1: Backward steps

NEED:

Papers []
Writing tools []

Talk about determination and discuss how being aware of all the steps we need to take can give us a better chance of finishing what we start.

At the bottom of your paper write down a goal that you have. Something simple that you want to create, achieve, or learn. At the top, write down the word "START".

Write 10 steps that can help you go from START all the way to reaching your goal. Assign an amount of time to each step or a date by which you can accomplish that step. Are there steps you can speed up? Are there steps you can skip? Do you think writing these steps can help you accomplish your goal?

Activity 2: What else could it be?

Discuss together how being persistent and determined can allow us to see things differently sometimes. Place all the objects in front of everyone and have each person or each group choose an object. Either individually or in teams, have everyone invent new uses and names for the items. Present to the group.

NEED:

Different objects
(the weirder the better) []

Discuss how easy or hard it was to look at objects differently and whether determination and persistence made a difference in the number of uses you found.

Ways to practice Determination:

💜 Try to finish what you start, no matter how hard it may seem.

💜 Finish reading a book.

💜 Write a story with a beginning, middle and end.

💜 Try to learn a new language or a new sport.

6. Forgiveness

True or False - Discuss your choices:

We show forgiveness when we tell others
that we are sorry even if we don't really mean it.
True [ ] False [ ]

Forgiveness is a quality that allows us to have
understanding, patience and love for other
people when they make mistakes.
True [ ] False [ ]

When we forgive someone, we should no
longer feel angry at them. We are able to
listen to what they have to say and accept
their apologies.
True [ ] False [ ]

If we make a mistake, we should try to
hide it and make sure we run away before
others can see who has made the mistake.
True [ ] False [ ]

A beautiful quote about Forgiveness:

Write down a quote that you wish
to memorize or remember.
If you cannot find a quote to inspire you,
try coming up with your own.

Word Game:

Colour the words that show examples of Forgiveness and discuss your choices.
Create sentences that show Forgiveness using some of these words or combinations.

SHOW MERCY	MAKE A CARD	SAY SORRY
COOK	UNDERSTAND	WALK OUTSIDE
DANCE	KNIT	EAT

Come up with an example of someone practicing Forgiveness.

Activity 1: Forgiveness heart

NEED:
Large Papers []
Writing and colouring tools []

Cut out a big heart and inside the heart write down different things that have happened recently that have made you angry or upset. Write as many things as possible in different sections of the heart. Decide whether or not you will forgive all the people for all the things that have happened.
If you decide NOT to forgive someone, then rip the section of the heart with the details of what you do not wish to forgive. If you decide to forgive the people who did something to you, then leave those sections of the heart in.
How does your heart look at the end?
Discuss what it means when you decide not to forgive someone.
Discuss how hard or easy it is to forgive and what do you gain by forgiving someone.

Activity 2: Create a play (drama)
No material

Act out the following scene and come up with your own ending:
Have different people act out different roles.

In this play, 2 friends notice a box filled with candy while visiting a store.
They decide to steal some candy. They get caught by the owner of the store.
Decide what happens next.
Decide whether or not the store owner should forgive the two friends.
Discuss how hard it is sometimes to forgive people for their mistakes.

Decide if the friends could do something to show how sorry they are.

Ways to practice Forgiveness:

💜 Take the habit of saying "I'm sorry" when you make a mistake.

💜 Forgive someone for something they have done to you.

💜 Make apology cards when you make mistakes.

💜 Look at things from someone else's point of view.

7. Generosity

True or False - Discuss your choices:

Generosity means giving everything away and not keeping anything for yourself.
True [ ] False [ ]

Generosity makes us want to share what we have with the people we love as well as with those who have less than us.
True [ ] False [ ]

We can learn to be generous by sharing what we have, giving things away when others don't have anything, or opening our hearts and our homes to others.
True [ ] False [ ]

You need to have a lot of things in order to be generous.
True [ ] False [ ]

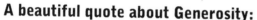

A beautiful quote about Generosity:
Write down a quote that you wish to memorize or remember. If you cannot find a quote to inspire you, try coming up with your own.

Word Game:
Colour the words that show examples of Generosity and discuss your choices.
Create sentences that show Generosity using some of these words or combinations.

BE KIND	PLAY HOUSE	BE CHARITABLE
PUSH	SHARE	GO HIDE
READ A BOOK	JUMP	RECEIVE

Come up with an example of someone practicing Generosity.

Activity 1: Share laughter

Sometimes sharing a good joke can be just as nice as sharing something you have. It makes everyone happy. Learn a few good jokes and share them with people you love. Make sure that the jokes you learn are not offensive to anyone. Make a nice card by folding a paper in half for someone with a fun saying on the front and write one of your favourite jokes inside. What a nice way to share laughter!
Talk to your friends and family and see what jokes you can share.

NEED:
Writing tools []
Papers []
Colouring tools []

Activity 2: Create a Generosity Journal

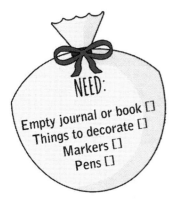

NEED:
Empty journal or book []
Things to decorate []
Markers []
Pens []

A generosity journal is a journal or book where you record experiences of generosity. You can share some of your generous actions or stories of other people being generous. The purpose is to encourage generosity by sharing these beautiful stories and experiences. Before you write anything inside, decorate the journal in a nice and creative way.

On the first page, write down what a generosity journal is in your words. Write how after each story, the journal will be passed on to someone else. This will give a chance to share a story of generosity.

When you have completed decorating and you have written what a generosity journal is, share your own generosity story in the journal. You can also include something small to share with others. Give the journal to someone else and ask them to write in it too.

Ways to practice Generosity:

💜 Share something you love with your family.

💜 Volunteer some of your time. It doesn't have to be a big job, something as simple as doing something nice for a neighbour or a friend.

💜 Go through your clothes and toys and see if there are things you can give away to others.

💜 Bake cookies for someone you love.

8. Gentleness

True or False - Discuss your choices:

Gentleness is how we do things in a very caring, and careful manner.
True [ ] False [ ]

We always need to do our best to be gentle and kind with everyone.
True [ ] False [ ]

We can use a gentle voice and be gentle in how we do things. We can also be gentle by thinking of others and doing nice things for them.
True [ ] False [ ]

We should never be gentle with people who have been mean to us.
True [ ] False [ ]

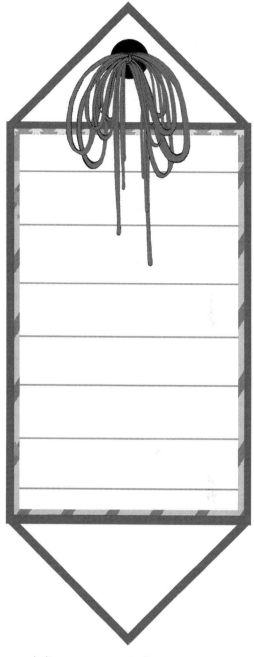

A beautiful quote about Gentleness:

Write down a quote that you wish to memorize or remember.
If you cannot find a quote to inspire you, try coming up with your own.

Word Game:
Colour the words that show examples of Gentleness and discuss your choices.
Create sentences that show Gentleness using some of these words or combinations.

BE TENDER	READ	BE LAZY
DRINK WATER	PLAY ROUGH	PAINT
BE PEACEFUL	TALK SOFTLY	MAKE A MESS

Come up with an example of someone practicing Gentleness.

Activity 1: Character description - Gentle person

NEED:
Drawing
or painting tools []
Papers []
Writing tools []

If I told you someone was a very gentle, what would that mean to you?

What would they look like?
Discuss what type of things they would do as a gentle person?
What would they wear?
What would they do for a hobby?
What would they smell like?
What would they eat?
What would others think of them?

Come up with a description as complete as you possibly can and make an drawing
or painting of this character. Make a second drawing of yourself as a gentle person.

Activity 2: Gentle art

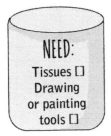

NEED:
Tissues []
Drawing
or painting
tools []

Discuss times when you have to be very gentle in your actions.
Give everyone a couple of sheets of tissue and have everyone try to draw
or paint on the tissues without tearing them.

Share the results together and discuss what skills
you had to use to avoid tearing your tissues.

Discuss other ways we can practice gentleness.

Ways to practice Gentleness:

♥ Practice being gentle with younger children and with small animals.

♥ Try being very quiet when it's time to do quiet things.

♥ Sing songs very gently to help someone fall asleep.

♥ Help with difficult and precise tasks.

9. Helpfulness

True or False - Discuss your choices:

We are helpful when we boss others around
and yell at them.
True [ ] False [ ]

We are helpful when we do things to help others
and make life easier for them.
True [ ] False [ ]

You have to be strong or very old to be helpful.
Young people cannot be helpful.
True [ ] False [ ]

When you are asked to be helpful,
you should say no and run away as fast as possible.
True [ ] False [ ]

A beautiful quote about Helpfulness:
Write down a quote that you wish
to memorize or remember.
If you cannot find a quote to inspire you,
try coming up with your own.

Word Game:
Colour the words that show examples of Helpfulness and discuss your choices.
Create sentences that show Helpfulness using some of these words or combinations.

SHOW YOU CARE	EAT MORE FOOD	SHOUT
COOPERATE	GO SHOPPING	BE KIND
DANCE	VOLUNTEER	SUPPORT

Come up with an example of someone practicing Helpfulness.

Activity 1: Different ways to help
No material

Come up with different scenarios together. Think about scenarios in which someone might need help doing something. Start acting the scenes out but stop just before offering help. Stand still and have someone else come in the scene and complete the scene showing how they can be helpful. Start over as many times as you can, each time completing the scene in a different way. Make sure everyone gets a turn acting out different roles. Discuss how each one of us can be helpful in everyday life.

Activity 2: These are the ways I can help

NEED:
Cardboard []
Writing tools []
Markers []

Come up with ten different ways you can help someone else. Be as specific as you can. Think of what you like to do, but mostly what would really be helpful to someone else. Using the cardboard, make a card to give to someone who might need your help. Give it to them before they ask for help.

On the front of the card write something like (use your own words) "I know how hard you have been working, I would like to help."

On the inside of the card, write your list of what you can do and next to that have a box that can be checked. Write something like "Please check 5 (you decide on the number) things that I can help with. Make sure you follow through with what you have offered to help with on the card.

Discuss what would be the appropriate attitude when being helpful.

Share how the world might be different if we were all a little more helpful.

Ways to practice Helpfulness:

❤ When you think someone might need your help, offer it joyfully.

❤ Do something nice for someone without them knowing about it.

❤ Always say "thank you" and "you're welcome."

❤ Help with cleaning around the house, setting the table, or other services.

10. Honesty

True or False - Discuss your choices:

Honesty means telling the truth and doing what we believe is right.
True [ ] False [ ]

It's okay not to keep your promise or tell the truth.
True [ ] False [ ]

Honest people always make an effort to be fair and just.
True [ ] False [ ]

If you have nothing nice to say, it's better not to say anything at all.
True [ ] False [ ]

A beautiful quote about Honesty:

Write down a quote that you wish
to memorize or remember.
If you cannot find a quote to inspire you,
try coming up with your own.

Word Game:

Colour the words that show examples of Honesty and discuss your choices.
Create sentences that show Honesty using some of these words or combinations.

LYING	JUMPING	BEING TRUTHFUL
BEING SINCERE	SAYING SORRY	MAKING A CARD
GOING OUTSIDE	MAKING STUFF UP	SEWING

Come up with an example of someone practicing Honesty.

Activity 1: Finish the story

NEED:
Papers □
Writing
tools □

Read the beginning of Jay's story and come up with 3 different ways
of finishing the story. Discuss the different possibilities together, and
share your own experiences in finding lost objects.

Jay's story:

Jay could not believe his luck. He was riding around on his old bike when he first saw it.
Lying on the ground was a brand new wallet. He opened it quickly and found a handful of
new twenty dollar bills along with cards and other less interesting things. There was
more than enough for the new bike he had always wanted.

He thought for a second about his choices...

Choice 1   **Choice 2**   **Choice 3**

Activity 2: Broken telephone

NEED:
Papers □
Scissors □
Writing
tools □

Discuss together the effect of backbiting and telling lies. Cut small pieces
of paper so that each person gets one piece. On most of the papers write
tell the truth. On one paper write **exaggerate**. On another write **lie** and
on another paper write **make something up**. Feel free to add other things.

Fold all the papers and have everyone pick one randomly. Make sure no one
shares what they have picked. Explain that each person will have to pass on
the information they receive using the instructions on their paper. Have one person whisper
something about himself or herself in the next person's ear. Depending on what they have
picked, the next person will either repeat it truthfully or do what their paper says.

Guess whether the information was changed or not at the end. Give everyone a chance to be at
the beginning of the line. Share together how it felt to have the information changed or added to.

Ways to practice Honesty:

♥ Don't lie and do your best to keep your promises. If you cannot keep a promise, explain why.

♥ When playing games, follow the rules and make sure you are all playing fair.

♥ Return something that you found.

11. Joyfulness

True or False - Discuss your choices:

Being joyful means being happy and wanting to share that joy and happiness with others.
True [ ] False [ ]

If you are joyful then you can never be sad, you must always be happy.
True [ ] False [ ]

When we are joyful we are full of love and we want to do things to make others happy.
True [ ] False [ ]

When we are joyful we want to have fun and share laughter with others.
True [ ] False [ ]

A beautiful quote about Joyfulness:
Write down a quote that you wish
to memorize or remember.
If you cannot find a quote to inspire you,
try coming up with your own.

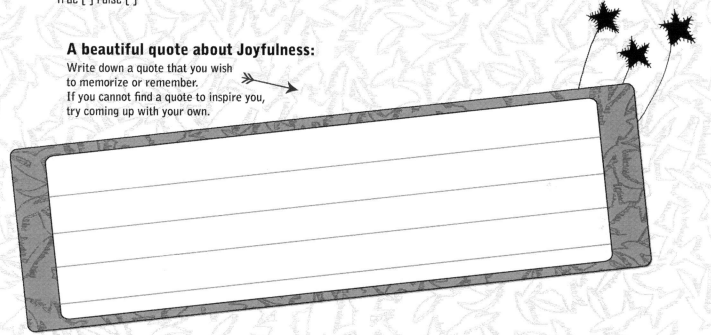

Word Game:
Colour the words that show examples of Joyfulness and discuss your choices.
Create sentences that show Joyfulness using some of these words or combinations.

BE ANGRY	BE CONFIDENT	BE CHEERFUL
BE A BEE	BE HAPPY	BE SMART
BE NICE	BE JOYOUS	BE MAD

Come up with an example of someone practicing Joyfulness.

Activity 1: Exploring Joyfulness

Write a poem or make a drawing/painting that shows an abstract expression of joyfulness. Abstract means that it does not have to represent anything real. Think of these sentence starters as inspiration in creating your art or poem. Put your art or poem somewhere where it will bring joy in your life.

Joyfulness comes in shades of ...

It smells like ...

You find it...

It tastes like...

It looks like...

Activity 2: Happiness can/box

Decorate the outside of the can (or box) with people and things you are happy to have around you. Draw the images out on paper, colour them and glue them onto the outside of the can (or box). On a separate piece of paper write down as many things as you can think of that make you happy. Cut them up and place them inside your can. When you are feeling sad, take a look at your happiness can (or box) or take out a reminder of what makes you happy.

Ways to practice Joyfulness:

♥ Have fun. Laughter and joy are contagious.

♥ Do at least one thing a week that is a little silly but a lot of fun.

♥ Have a laughing contest with your family or your friends.

♥ Watch a funny movie with your family.

♥ Have a party for no reason. Sing and dance.

12. Kindness

True or False - Discuss your choices:

Kindness means letting others push you around.
True [ ] False [ ]

Kindness means caring and doing nice things for others.
True [ ] False [ ]

We are kind when we take care of animals and do our best to make others happy.
True [ ] False [ ]

You should never be kind. Others may ask you to do things for them.
True [ ] False [ ]

A beautiful quote about Kindness:
Write down a quote that you wish to memorize or remember.
If you cannot find a quote to inspire you, try coming up with your own.

Word Game:
Colour the words that show examples of Kindness and discuss your choices.
Create sentences that show Kindness using some of these words or combinations.

SHOW MERCY	CARE	EXERCISE
WORK HARD	HELP OTHERS	SHARE
RUN FAST	WEAR A HAT	EAT FAST

Come up with an example of someone practicing Kindness.

Activity 1: Album of kind acts

Fold 3 or 4 large papers in half to make an album of about 6 to 8 pages. Staple together on one side as if you are making a book. On each page of the album draw a picture frame and draw different acts of kindness. These can be acts that you have done or examples of kindness. You can also cut pictures out of magazines or use actual photos and place them in the album. Decorate your album and share it with others. Discuss what you see in the newspaper and in magazines in general and whether or not you feel there are enough acts of kindness in the world.

NEED:
Large papers []
Writing tools []
Colouring tools []
Magazines []
Stapler []
Glue []

What would help make people kinder to each other?

Activity 2: My friends and I

NEED:
Papers []
Writing tools []

Discuss how being kind also means being a good friend. Share the qualities you need to have in order to be a good friend. Draw a table with three columns. In the first column write the names of some of your friends. In the second column write down something positive about each person (it could be something about who they are, or what they do well). In the last column write down something you can do for each person that will help make your friendship stronger.

Ways to practice Kindness:

♥ Be kind to people and animals.

♥ Be generous and charitable. Share what you have with those who have less than you.

♥ Have a "do something nice" day in your family on which everyone does something kind.

♥ Read or write a story about someone being kind.

13. Moderation

True or False - Discuss your choices:

We practice moderation by trying to create balance in our lives.
True [ ] False [ ]

Moderation means that we make an effort not to have too much or too little of things, but just the right amount.
True [ ] False [ ]

You can never have too much of something you love.
True [ ] False [ ]

Being moderate means you can never have anything you love.
True [ ] False [ ]

A beautiful quote about Moderation:

Write down a quote that you wish to memorize or remember. If you cannot find a quote to inspire you, try coming up with your own.

Word Game:

Colour the words that show examples of Moderation and discuss your choices.
Create sentences that show Moderation using some of these words or combinations.

BE MODERATE	APPRECIATE	SHOW CONTROL
WANT MORE	BRAG	EAT RAW FOODS
THINK	MAKE GOOD CHOICES	TAKE A BATH

Come up with an example of someone practicing Moderation.

Activity 1: Catalogue of useless things

NEED:
Papers []
Writing tools []
Colouring tools []
Magazines []
Scissors []
Glue or tape []
Stapler []

Discuss how much is too much and how we are often tempted to want more and more things. Discuss whether things make us better people or not. Fold a few sheets of paper in half and staple them in the middle to create a catalogue of things that are useless or that you personally don't need. You can create different categories such as **things that only make you want more** or **things we don't need**. Come up with as many categories as you want. Go through magazines to find certain images, draw others, or write about them. Discuss how you feel when you go through your catalogue and whether or not possessions make you who you are. Discuss what adds value to your life.

Activity 2: What Moderation looks like

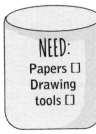

NEED:
Papers []
Drawing tools []

Draw a person in the center of your sheet of paper. On the left side write the words TOO LITTLE and on the right side, the words TOO MUCH. Think of different things that could influence the way your person may look and act, for example, if he or she had TOO LITTLE food or TOO MUCH food. Draw your character in as many scenarios as possible.

Discuss the importance of moderation.
How can we show moderation when there are so many things around?
How can us practicing moderation balance some of the injustices in the world?

Ways to practice Moderation:

❤Think about what happens when you don't practice moderation in eating.

❤Look at all your toys and the things that you have and decide if there are things you can give away to people who have less.

❤Develop your own identity. Be unique.
Realize that you don't need to have things just because other people have them.

14. Modesty

True or False - Discuss your choices:

We show modesty by respecting
ourselves and others.
True [ ] False [ ]

Modesty means not bragging about
something that we are proud of and
making ourselves seem better than others.
True [ ] False [ ]

Modesty means choosing what we wear
and how we look so that we are respectful,
clean and appropriately dressed.
True [ ] False [ ]

Being modest means wearing fashionable
clothes and looking like everyone else.
True [ ] False [ ]

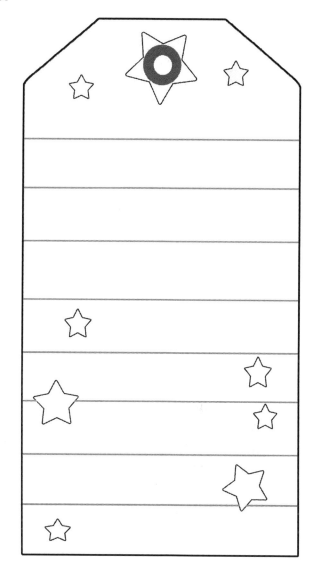

A beautiful quote about Modesty:

Write down a quote that you wish
to memorize or remember.
If you cannot find a quote to inspire you,
try coming up with your own.

Word Game:
Colour the words that show examples of Modesty and discuss your choices.
Create sentences that show Modesty using some of these words or combinations.

DRESS UP	BE HUMBLE	BE PROUD
MAKE CHOICES	UNDERSTAND	BE LOUD
FOLLOW OTHERS	SHOW RESPECT	GET MOVING

Come up with an example of someone practicing Modesty.

Activity 1: Finish the stories

Finish the following stories in ways that show the characters being modest about their physical appearance or their accomplishments. If you think of more than one way to finish the stories, have more than one ending. Share the completed stories.

NEED:
Writing tools []
Papers []

1. Sophie looked at the store window and stared at the super short pink and silver mini skirt. She didn't like wearing clothes that we so short and tight but everyone was wearing these skirts at school and she loved the colours of the skirt. All her friends had one and she had saved up for months to buy herself some new clothes ...

2. Sasha arrived at his friend's birthday party. There was music and food and it was a lot of fun. Towards the end of the party, his friend decided he wanted to play a kissing game. Sasha didn't know what to do because he didn't want to play the game and did not feel it was right. He was afraid of never being invited to a party again if he didn't play...

3. After months of practice and hard work, the basketball team finally won the semi-finals and was headed to the final game of the season. Tina was extremely proud of herself at the end of the game. She had scored the most points and she felt that this was her best game yet. As she met the rest of the girls in the locker room, she...

Activity 2: Ad Alert

NEED:
Fashion magazines []
Markers []
Writing tools []
Papers []

Look through a fashion magazine and read a couple of articles. With a marker, circle everything that DOES NOT show a good example of modesty. Choose a picture or an article and change it to create or show a positive message instead.
Discuss what messages different magazines send.
Who do you feel the message is targeting?
What kind of messages would you rather see instead?

Ways to practice Modesty:

❤When playing games, think about how you need to act if you win or lose and how bragging makes others feel.

❤Look at how other people dress and think about some of their choices. Think about what choices you can make about the way you dress.

15. Patience

True or False - Discuss your choices:

We show that we are patient when we get angry at others for being late.
True [ ] False [ ]

We show that we can be patient when we wait for something or someone without being angry or upset or when we don't make others feel bad for being late.
True [ ] False [ ]

We can show patience by taking the time to do something well instead of rushing through it.
True [ ] False [ ]

We show that we are patient by doing things very fast, even if they are not done properly.
True [ ] False [ ]

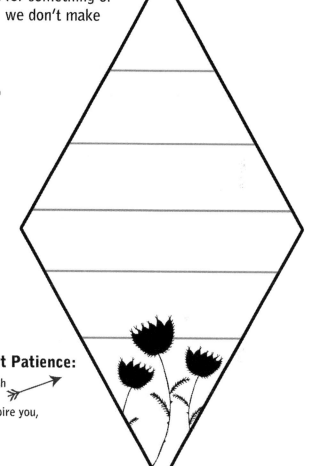

A beautiful quote about Patience:

Write down a quote that you wish to memorize or remember.
If you cannot find a quote to inspire you, try coming up with your own.

Word Game:

Colour the words that show examples of Patience and discuss your choices.
Create sentences that show Patience using some of these words or combinations.

WAIT	BE BORED	SING A SONG
COOK	UNDERSTAND	WALK OUTSIDE
READ A NOVEL	BE TOLERANT	RUN FAST

Come up with an example of someone practicing Patience.

Activity 1: Inside myself

Discuss how being patient is part of life and has an important role in everything we do. Tape several papers together to create one large paper. Lie down on your large paper and have someone else trace your outline. Help each other in the process.

Once you have the outline, write the word PATIENCE where your heart would be. Write or draw other things that can help you be more patient. Think about skills, virtues, or qualities that make you unique and patient.

Activity 2: Role reversal

Discuss how sometimes we can be very impatient with others. We don't always know what it is like to be in their shoes or do what they have to do. Choose someone in your family or a friend that you may have been impatient towards. Together, make a list of what you would normally do for the next half hour. Reverse roles. You become them and they become you. You must go through the list and do what the other person would normally be doing. How does it feel to be someone else?

After 30 minutes, share if you feel more patient and understanding towards them.

Ways to practice Patience:

♥ Create a small reminder that you can say to yourself when you find it hard to be patient.

♥ Bring things to keep yourself occupied when you have to wait for a long time.

♥ Think about how helpful you can be simply by being patient.

♥ Try to see it from the other person's point of view.

16. Respect

True or False - Discuss your choices:

We show respect when we listen to loud music even if others are trying to sleep.
True [ ] False [ ]

Respect is how we show that we care and appreciate things and people.
True [ ] False [ ]

We can show respect for the environment by doing our best to care for it. We can show that we respect others by being polite and behaving in a nice way towards them.
True [ ] False [ ]

We show respect by not listening to others and using bad words when we talk.
True [ ] False [ ]

A beautiful quote about Respect:

Write down a quote that you wish to memorize or remember.
If you cannot find a quote to inspire you, try coming up with your own.

Word Game:

Colour the words that show examples of Respect and discuss your choices.
Create sentences that show Respect using some of these words or combinations.

LISTEN	SHOUT	APOLOGIZE
DANCE	SHARE	SNORE
BE POLITE	PUSH	ADMIRE

Come up with an example of someone practicing Respect.

Activity 1: Alien encounter

Imagine that you have just spent a couple of days visiting an alien planet as a special guest representing earth. You must now hand in your report describing your experience.

Write down what the planet looks like, what the aliens look like, what they wear and what they eat. Talk about their customs and how they reacted to your customs. Explain how you behaved to show respect for their culture. Share your report with others.

Discuss how different cultures should respect each other.

Activity 2: Image talking

NEED:

Magazines []
Scissors []
Glue or tape []
Papers []

Discuss what self-respect means and how we practice it by the way we choose to dress. Talk about assumptions people make by looking at how others dress. Find a magazine, newspaper or catalogue in your house. A fashion magazine may work best. Go through it and discuss what you see. Find five images that send a positive message. Discuss each image and the choices the person has made when it comes to showing self-respect. Cut the images out and glue or tape them on a separate piece of paper. Share the choices you make to show self-respect.

Ways to practice Respect:

❤ Be respectful towards other people no matter how they act towards you.

❤ Think about ways you can show respect for your grandparents.

❤ Listen to the people who care for you.

❤ Watch what you say.

17. Responsibility

True or False - Discuss your choices:

Being responsible means doing what is necessary to take care
of the people and things we love.
True [ ] False [ ]

When we are responsible, others know that they can trust us.
True [ ] False [ ]

We are responsible when we lie and don't keep our promises.
True [ ] False [ ]

We can show we are responsible by taking good care of the environment.
True [ ] False [ ]

A beautiful quote about Responsibility: Write down a quote that you wish to memorize or remember. If you cannot find a quote to inspire you, try coming up with your own.

Word Game:

Colour the words that show examples of Responsibility and discuss your choices.
Create sentences that show Responsibility using some of these words or combinations.

BLAME OTHERS	MAKE A CARD	TAKE CARE
MAKE FACES	BE TRUSTWORTHY	WALK OUTSIDE
DO A GOOD JOB	BE LAZY	BE RELIABLE

Come up with an example of someone practicing Responsibility.

Activity 1: Create your own advertisement

NEED:
Papers []
Colouring tools []
Posters []
Large box []
Scissors []

Pretend you are responsible for making an advertisement to promote responsibility. You can decide whether you only want to focus on the environment or if you want to talk about other aspects of being responsible. Cut part of the box out to turn it into a television. Write your advertisement down and research statistics to make it more accurate if you want. Use the poster and papers to create props for your presentation. Practice your advertisement before presenting it to others. Discuss whether or not you liked creating this type of advertisement and how you can help share important messages through the media.

Activity 2: Interview someone about responsibilities

Find someone older than you (a lot older if possible) and ask them the following questions about responsibility or come up with your own questions:

NEED:
Someone to interview []
Papers []
Writing tools []

1. How would you define responsibilities?
2. What is the benefit of being responsible?
3. When you were young, what type of responsibilities did you have?
4. When you think back about all the responsibilities you had, which one was the most important? Why?
5. Do you think kids today are more or less responsible than when you were young? Why?
6. What do you think are some other qualities people must have in order to be responsible?

Once you have your answers, share your responses with others and discuss how you would answer some of these questions.

Ways to practice Responsibility:

💜 Look at what responsibilities you have and try your best to show that you can be trusted.

💜 As you get older, show that you can be responsible for more things.
Be proud of being given more responsibilities.

💜 Think about ways of being responsible for the planet.

18. Service

True or False - Discuss your choices:

You have to be really strong to
do a service for someone else.
True [ ] False [ ]

Doing a service for someone else
is like having a job where you
don't get paid.
True [ ] False [ ]

Being of service is what we do
when we help others.
True [ ] False [ ]

We can be of service by being helpful
when others need help as well as by
being caring and kind.
True [ ] False [ ]

A beautiful quote about Service:
Write down a quote that you wish
to memorize or remember.
If you cannot find a quote to inspire you,
try coming up with your own.

Word Game:
Colour the words that show examples of Service and discuss your choices.
Create sentences that show Service using some of these words or combinations.

COOK	UNDERSTAND	HELP
DANCE	ASSIST OTHERS	YELL
VOLUNTEER	FEED YOUR PET	EAT

Come up with an example of someone practicing Service.

Activity 1: An afternoon service – cookies and time

*Feel free to use your own cookie recipe.

Discuss how sometimes being of service can mean spending time with someone and getting to know them better. With the help of an adult make cookies following these instructions. If you have other favourite cookies, make the ones you like. Decorate a box and put some napkins inside before putting in the cookies. Make a nice card for the person you plan to give them to and go over and give them the cookies. Spend time talking to them and sitting with them if they invite you to. Get to know them.

Preheat oven to 375° F and line cookie sheets with wax paper. If you don't have any wax (or parchment) paper, oil your cookie sheet.

Combine flour, cinnamon, baking soda, salt, your choice of nuts, quick oats and raisins in a medium sized bowl.

Beat the eggs and the vegetable oil in a different bowl. Mix in the teaspoon of vanilla extract.

Mix everything together.

Using a tablespoon, drop the cookie dough onto the baking sheet making sure to leave about an inch between each cookie.

Bake for about 8 to 10 minutes

Flour (1 Cup)	Cinnamon (1 teaspoon)
Baking soda (1 teaspoon)	Salt (1/2 teaspoon)
Your favourite nuts (1/2 Cup)	2 Eggs
Quick oats – not instant (1 Cup)	
Raisins or dried cranberries (1 Cup)	
Applesauce (1 Cup)	
Vegetable Oil (1/2 Cup)	Box or bag []
Vanilla Extract (1 teaspoon)	Napkins []

Let cool, enjoy and share.
Don't forget to clean up!

Activity 2: Making a difference

NEED:
Papers []
Writing tools []
Drawing tools []

If you think you are too small to make a difference, try sleeping in a room with a mosquito.
– African proverb

Discuss what you think this proverb means and how it applies to being of service. Come up with your own service project and make sure you follow through with your commitment! Here are some guidelines to make it more inspiring:
-Involve either your family or your friends.
-Give yourself a name, logo and mission (a mission can just be one sentence that narrows down what kind of service you want your group to focus on).
-Decide how much time you are willing to devote and make sure you set that time apart.
-Do some research about the needs of your community or neighborhood.
Have fun!

Ways to practice Service:

💜 Volunteer your time.

💜 Spend an afternoon in a home for the elderly.

19. Trust

True or False - Discuss your choices:

If you trust someone else, then you have to do everything they say.
True [ ] False [ ]

Trust is how people know they can count on us and we can count on them.
True [ ] False [ ]

We can show that we can be trusted by caring for others, by taking good care of what people lend us, and by being responsible.
True [ ] False [ ]

We can show that we can be trusted by keeping our promises.
True [ ] False [ ]

A beautiful quote about Trust:

Write down a quote that you wish to memorize or remember.
If you cannot find a quote to inspire you, try coming up with your own.

Word Game:

Colour the words that show examples of Trust and discuss your choices.
Create sentences that show Trust using some of these words or combinations.

BE RELIABLE	MAKE A CARD	SAY A POEM
KEEP YOUR WORD	BELIEVE OTHERS	TELL A SECRET
FLY A KITE	GET A HAIRCUT	BE RESPONSIBLE

Come up with an example of someone practicing Trust.

Activity 1: Short story about trust

NEED:
Papers []
Writing tools []
Drawing tools []

Come up with your own definition of what it means to trust someone else. Write a short story in which the main character has to trust someone else to do something very important. Have different endings if you can. Illustrate your story and share it with someone you trust.

Try to use 4 of these words in your story. If you don't know certain words, look them up:

TRUST	*BELIEVE*	*RELY ON*
EXPECTATION	*DEPEND*	*HOPE*
CONFIDENCE	*ASSUME*	*RESPONSIBLE*

Activity 2: What happens when?

NEED:
Different foods, (sweet, bitter, sour...) []
Blindfold []

Have everyone look at the snacks on the table. Blindfold one person and have someone else feed that person. The blindfolded person will ask for something that they want to try, but the other person will decide whether they will give the right snack or another snack. Discuss how it felt having to trust someone or being the person who was trusted. Make sure everyone gets to have the blindfold on. Have everyone involved in preparing the snacks and cleaning up afterwards.

Ways to practice Trust:

💜 Think about ways you can show that you can be trusted.

💜 When something happens, give others a chance to explain.

💜 Play games in which you have to trust someone and they have to trust you.

💜 Think about the consequences of your actions before you do them.

20. Unity

True or False - Discuss your choices:

We show unity when we make an effort to get along with other people and when we love them for their uniqueness and differences.
True [ ] False [ ]

Being united means having to do everything the same way as other people.
True [ ] False [ ]

Unity means working together, cooperating with others and sharing a common goal.
True [ ] False [ ]

Unity means everyone dressing the same way and speaking the same language.
True [ ] False [ ]

A beautiful quote about Unity:

Write down a quote that you wish to memorize or remember.
If you cannot find a quote to inspire you, try coming up with your own.

Word Game:

Colour the words that show examples of Unity and discuss your choices.
Create sentences that show Unity using some of these words or combinations.

LOVE	MUST BE RIGHT	PEACE
COLLABORATE	RESPECT	AGREE
CHOSE PEACE	PLAY BALL	FIGHT

Come up with an example of someone practicing Unity.

Activity 1: The colour of unity

NEED:
Large papers []
Colouring tools []
Paints []
Paintbrushes []

Make a line in the middle of your paper. On one side paint colours that you feel show unity. On the other side, paint what would represent the opposite of unity. Discuss how and why you came up with these colours or designs and what they represent to you.

Share what you can do to help contribute to the unity of the world.

Activity 2: Working machines

Working machines* are different small machines that you find around the house with visible working parts
(for example: egg beater, scissors, can opener, garlic press, music box, windup toy, pencil sharpener, stapler etc.)

NEED:
Papers []
Drawing tools []
Writing tools []
Working machines* []

Observe a machine closely from different angles. Examine how it works. Create three drawings of the machine you are observing.

In the first drawing, assume that one of the parts decides that it is more important than the others and should be much bigger. Draw that part bigger.

In the second drawing assume that half of the parts have decided that they no longer need the other half to function. Draw half of the machine.

In the last drawing draw only the parts that are necessary for the machine to function properly.

Share each of your drawings and how each part of the machine has a role. What does this show us about unity?

Ways to practice Unity:

♥ Get to know people who are different from you. Learn about their culture, their language and their habits.

♥ Do something with your family at least once a week. Play games, watch a movie together or have a nice family meal.

♥ Host a Unity Feast. Bring together your friends and family, have everyone bring some food and get to know each other better.

Write in the white space.

Decorate the space left.

Cut on the gray pattern.

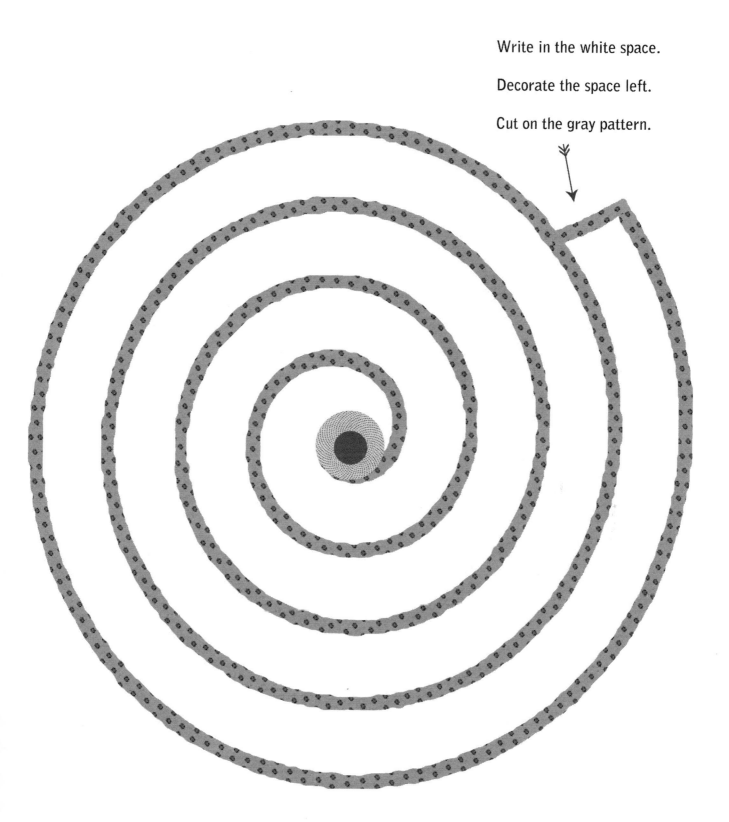

Make a hole in the center and hang using the string.

Nutritional Facts
per 175 g

Loyalty	5%
Courage	3%
Determination	4%
Sugar	7%
Responsibility	3%
Vitamine A	6%
Vitamine C	4%
Patience	8%
Kindness	4%
Compassion	3%
Proteins	1%
Love	6%
Self-discipline	13%
Respect	4%
Sucres	7%
Carbohydrates	0%
Vitamine D	6%
Vitamine E	4%
Trust	3%
Calcium	9%

Nutritional Facts
per

Directions:

Nutritional Facts
per

Directions:

Nutritional Facts
per

Directions:

Made in the USA
Columbia, SC
14 February 2021

32953637R00028